Contents

Introduction

During the 1930s the German leader Adolf Hitler started to build up a powerful army and then invade surrounding countries. First Austria fell to Germany in 1938 and the following year it was Czechoslovakia. On 1st September 1939 Hitler marched his troops into Poland. Britain and France challenged Hitler to withdraw and gave him a deadline of 11 a.m. on 3rd September.

⬇ Fighting a fire in London after one of the many air raids by German bombers.

WAR IS DECLARED

Hitler ignored the challenge and when the deadline passed, war against Germany was declared. The war lasted for six years and, during that time, most of the rest of the world became involved in what became known as World War II.

EVERYONE IS INVOLVED

Everyone who lived through World War II was affected by it in some way. Men who were not employed in vital jobs were called up to join the armed forces. Those who were not able to fight joined voluntary groups. Women also joined the armed forces, did voluntary work or went to work in schools, hospitals or factories and carried out many other vital tasks. Everyone had to survive on limited food rations.

PULLING TOGETHER

Although Britain was not invaded by enemy troops, civilians suffered bombing raids night after night. Many thousands of people were killed. For their safety children were evacuated from the cities to the countryside and were often separated from their parents for long periods. It was a time when everyone in the country pulled together to join in 'the war effort' and to do their bit for victory.

WORLD WAR II

Sally Hewitt

W

This edition 2010

Franklin Watts
338 Euston Road
London NW1 3BH

Franklin Watts Australia
Level 17/207 Kent Street
Sydney, NSW 2000

Series editor: Sarah Peutrill
Series design: White Design
Art director: Jonathan Hair
Picture researcher: Diana Morris

A CIP catalogue record for this
book is available from the British Library

ISBN: 978 0 7496 9629 0
Dewey number: 940.5'3

Printed in Malaysia

Franklin Watts is a division of Hachette
Children's Books, an Hachette UK company.
www.hachette.co.uk

Picture Credits:
Central Press/Hulton Archive: 4, 10b, 15b; Croydon Times Ltd: front
cover b, 29cl; Express Newspapers/Hulton Archive: 29tr; Fox/Hulton
Archive: front cover tl, 7t, 16b, 26b, 27b, 28b; Hulton Archive: front
cover cr, 9t, 13bc, 13cr, 21tr; Hulton Archive/Corbis: 6b, 12b;
Keystone/Hulton Archive: 8b, 9b, 17t, 23b; LFI/Hulton Archive:
19b; Peter Newark's Pictures: front cover bl, 11b, 13bl, 17c, 22bl,
23bl, 23tr, 23cb; Picture Post/Hulton Archive: 20t. Whilst every
attempt has been made to clear copyright should there be any inadvertent omission
please apply in the first instance to the publisher regarding rectification.

The author and publisher would
like to thank all those who contributed
their memories and personal photographs to this book.

THEY CAN REMEMBER

In this book six people share their memories of what it was like to live in Britain in World War II. They each have a story to tell in their own section, but they also add other memories throughout the book.

Cynthia Palmer

Cynthia lived in Worthing, Sussex, during the war. She remembers the day war was declared. She was 10 years old.

Bill Mellow

Bill was a naval commando during the war. He served his country all over the world.

Brian King

Brian was aged six and living in Essex when the war began. Soon after he was evacuated to Derbyshire.

Meg Stone

Meg remembers her time as a Land Army girl during the war working on farms in Hampshire, Berkshire, Warwickshire, and Shropshire.

Eileen Crewdson

Eileen was a child living on a farm in Herefordshire. She remembers how the war affected people in the country.

Amy Sumner

Amy worked at the Liverpool Telephone Exchange when war broke out. She joined the ATS in 1941.

5

The day war broke out

Cynthia, 1943

WORRYING TIMES

Cynthia lived on the south coast in Worthing, Sussex, in a seaside hotel run by her parents. At the beginning of September 1939, just after her tenth birthday, there was a worrying atmosphere at home.

" My parents had been whispering together and stopping when they saw me listening. No one was on holiday at the hotel – the times were too dangerous and uncertain for that. "

WAR IS DECLARED

At 11a.m. on Sunday 3rd September 1939, people all over Britain gathered around wireless (radio) sets to hear a broadcast by the Prime Minister, Neville Chamberlain. In Europe, the German dictator Adolf Hitler had ordered his troops to invade Poland. Britain and France were expected to make a strong stand against him.

" The whole family sat by the wireless in the hotel dining room. It was a beautiful, late summer day. I could see the sea sparkling in the sunlight through the open windows. "

← Families became used to listening to announcements made on the wireless throughout the war.

THE PRIME MINISTER'S SPEECH

"I am speaking to you from the Cabinet Room at 10 Downing Street. This morning the British Ambassador in Berlin handed the German Government a final note, stating that unless we heard from them by 11 o'clock that they were prepared at once to withdraw their troops from Poland, a state of war would exist between us. I have to tell you that no such undertaking has been received, and that consequently this country is at war with Germany."

→ The British Prime Minister, Neville Chamberlain, declared war on Germany in 1939. In 1940 Winston Churchill became Prime Minister.

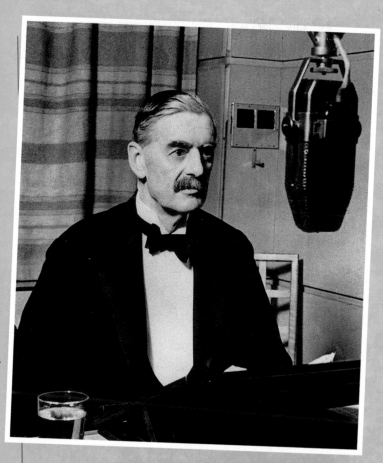

TEARS

" *I watched my parents standing very still with their arms around each other. My mother put her head on my father's shoulder and I saw tears running down her cheeks.* "

SIREN

" *Almost immediately the air was filled with a terrible wailing sound. We jumped up, terrified. I'd never heard a siren before, but my father knew what it was. He said, 'Keep calm everyone. It's an air raid.' He led us into the narrow passage next to the stairs where we huddled together for what seemed like eternity.* "

It was a false alarm. After 15 minutes the 'all-clear' sounded and Cynthia scrambled out into a world at war.

! Amy remembers...

"It was a Sunday and I was in Liverpool at home when I heard the news. At that time I had a boyfriend who was in the Royal Navy. I was very upset and I just cried – it was a crying time."

PHONEY WAR

At first, people experienced very little change in their daily lives so the first few months after war was declared became known as the 'phoney war'. But it wasn't long before the war became very real, affecting the lives of everyone in the country.

FRANCE SURRENDERS

Germany made swift progress in its campaign and France surrendered on 22 June 1940. This left only Britain to stand against Germany.

Living in danger

AIR RAIDS

The country prepared itself for air raids – bomb attacks by enemy aircraft, usually at night. At the first sign of approaching bombers, a siren would sound the warning for everyone to run for shelter. When the danger was over, another siren would sound the all-clear.

THE BLITZ 1940–41

The worst period was a continuous wave of bombing called the Blitz. The German bombers attacked homes as well military targets. Their aim was to break the spirit of the British people so that they would surrender. Instead, it made people more determined to fight back.

PROTECTION

People either built special air raid shelters, or took refuge in cellars, caves or tunnels such as the London Underground.

⬇ All over the country people built Anderson Shelters in their gardens so they could get to safety quickly.

ORDER NOW!!
YOUR
STEEL and CONCRETE
BOMB PROOF SHELTER
(As approved by the Government)

PROOF AGAINST ANYTHING OTHER THAN A DIRECT HIT

The whole Structure will be erected under Ground Level with a minimum of twelve inches of Concrete over. An Emergency Exit is also included.

ALL ORDERS WILL BE DEALT WITH IN STRICT ROTATION
but as we may have difficulty in obtaining materials you are advised to

PLACE YOUR ORDER IMMEDIATELY

PRICES ON APPLICATION
Come and inspect the Shelter we have just completed.

The London Underground sheltered thousands of people during air raids.

TRAGIC TIMES

People were not always able to reach safety and many thousands were killed in air raids across the country. Amy remembers the day that the Liverpool Telephone Exchange, where she worked, took a direct hit.

" I went down to work and the whole building had gone. Everyone had been killed. "

Gas masks

The government was afraid that poisonous gas as well as bombs would be dropped from the skies. Over 40 million gas masks were issued and people were meant to carry them with them all the time.

School children in 1941 try on their gas masks during a gas drill. Fortunately, Britain was not attacked by poisonous gas during World War II.

Evacuation

Brian King's story

OPERATION PIED PIPER

Between 1st and 3rd September 1939, in an operation named 'Pied Piper', nearly one and a half million people, most of them children, were moved out of cities to protect them from the expected bombing raids. They were sent to live in places that were thought to be safe, such as the countryside. This was called evacuation.

Brian, 1940

The government expected people to take evacuees into their homes as part of their contribution to what was called 'the war effort'.

Brian lived on the coast in Essex – an area where it was feared the Germans would land during an invasion. He was only six when he was evacuated to Derbyshire with the other children from his new school. He had to say goodbye to his mother at the station.

⬆ Brian and his mother walking to the station the day he was evacuated.

> " *I didn't know anybody from the school. We were taken on a long train journey to Ashbourne station where coaches were waiting for us. I remember being given a bag of barley sugars – I must have been sick of barley sugars at the end of it. And these coaches trundled round after a long train journey dropping children off. It was getting dark when we arrived at a little hamlet called Carsington.* "

⬅ Evacuation begins in September 1939. Police and railway staff at Ealing Broadway Station, London help young children on their way.

Local people arrived to choose their evacuees.

> *Since I was one of the younger boys – most of the older boys and girls were picked because they would be useful on the farm and could help with the washing and other jobs – I was left.*

At last, a couple took Brian home to their tiny 300-year-old cottage.

> *They were very kind people. They already had two daughters who were sleeping in their bedroom and a son, John, who was sleeping in a bed on the landing. I shared John's bed – we slept top to toe.*
>
> *I remember my first evening. I just cried and cried. They offered me green jelly – they thought it was a treat.*

Brian (left) with his evacuee family, outside the cottage.

LEAVE THIS TO US SONNY – **YOU** OUGHT TO BE OUT OF LONDON

MINISTRY OF HEALTH EVACUATION SCHEME

Poster campaigns

The government used posters to advise people during the war. They often used slogans that were easy to remember such as 'Dig for Victory' and 'Careless Talk Costs Lives'.

SAVING LIVES

In many cases, parents collected their children and took them home after only a short spell away. But if it hadn't been for evacuation, many more children would have died during the air raids.

Children at war

EVERYONE IS AFFECTED

The war changed daily life for everyone all over the country, even the children. Families were split up, homes were destroyed in air raids and there were shortages of almost everything from petrol to food.

BOARDING SCHOOL

Eileen was at boarding school and she remembers how the war affected the lives of her friends.

> " Lots of the girls at the school had parents in the services and sometimes, sadly, they were killed or taken prisoner. Other girls who lived in London or Birmingham had their homes bombed. Some lost their homes twice. "

SOUVENIRS

Some children found a new hobby – collecting war souvenirs – even though it was strictly forbidden.

Bill remembers his boat limping back from an operation into Shoreham harbour with a leak, and being besieged by local boys looking for souvenirs.

> " The young boys were there, they saw all the empty cartridges and they said, 'Can we have some of those?' and I said, 'Yes,' and gave them all these empty cartridges. "

! Cynthia remembers...

"If a plane had been shot down, the local boys went out to hunt for souvenirs from the wreckage. If anyone in authority found a boy with one of these souvenirs, he would be in trouble and it would be taken away from him."

↧ Collecting empty cartridges was a popular hobby.

WORK FOR EVERYONE

During Brian's evacuation he and the other children were given work to do.

> We had to walk down the village past a farm to which our cottage was attached and draw water from a well. We had a yoke with buckets that didn't fit children.

Across the country people were encouraged to 'Dig for Victory' – grow their own foods to relieve national food shortages. Vegetables were planted in every available piece of earth – in parks, gardens and even on railway embankments.

Food rationing

Imported foods such as sugar, tea and oranges became scarce as the German navy tried to sink supply ships. To give everyone a fair share of the food available, ration books were issued. In some cases, this meant that people ate better during the war than they had done before.

DIG ON FOR VICTORY

① Cynthia remembers...
"My mother said – sweet rationing is a good thing. You'll have healthier skin and teeth! But my brother and I didn't agree."

← The government encouraged everyone to 'Dig for Victory'.

Eileen, 1940

WAR COMES TO THE COUNTRYSIDE

Eileen was six when war broke out. Her family owned a farm in Herefordshire. It wasn't long before the war started to affect their lives, even in the heart of the countryside. Soldiers arrived during the first winter to operate searchlights trying to pick out enemy aircraft in the night sky.

AIR RAIDS AND FLYING COWS

Herefordshire had some of the first air raids as the Germans tried to bomb a munitions factory in Hereford.

> *One woman farmer was in bed when her farm was hit and then her house was machine-gunned. Fortunately, she was lying down in bed – the bed head had bullet holes in it. One of her cows landed on the other side of the house, none the worse for it – no one knows how!*

MYSTERIOUS EXPERIMENTS

The bombing became so bad that Eileen was sent away to boarding school where they had an air raid shelter with bunks to sleep in. But in nearby Malvern mysterious experiments were taking place. Later, Eileen found out that ways of confusing German radar were being tried out.

Eileen and her horse, Nutty

> *Sometimes masses of strips of silver paper were dropped. They fell in the grounds of the school and on the commons and hills. Sometimes they dropped loo paper, which unrolled in the air and caught in the trees. We made Christmas decorations from the silver paper.*

PRISONERS OF WAR

Many prisoners of war (POWs) were put to work on the farms. Saverio, an Italian prisoner aged 21, came to live on Eileen's farm and they became friends.

> " *Saverio helped ensure we had enough cut wood for the fire. He used to take me riding at the weekends and we went for miles. He used to sing opera arias.* "

After the war several Italian prisoners married local girls and did not return home.

→ Meg's letter, which is now in London's Imperial War Museum.

⬇ Italian Prisoners of War at work in the English countryside.

❗ Meg remembers...

"When I was working on a farm near Cheltenham, I had to bicycle to my job. A lorry overtook me full of prisoners of war. I used to cut them dead, obviously. It was my duty wasn't it? They were foreigners, they were Germans for heaven's sake! They were killing my brothers off! They used to wave at me and then one day I thought, 'Don't be such a stuffy old thing!' and I waved back. One day something was thrown out of the lorry and it was a little bit of paper. I got off my bike and picked it up. It was a letter."

Dear Girl!

It is very wrong from you, that we have a long time nothing seen from you. We are always very glad, when we can see you nicely face. — Dear Girl, we have an ask for you, can you drive now always along our bus. We are very happy, you allways to see. —

With the hope you can read this letter, and that we can you see allways in the next time, want we to shut.

You happy P. o. W.'s.

THE WAR EFFORT

Everyone was encouraged to do their bit for the war effort in whatever way they could. Those who were unfit, too young or too old to join the army, navy or air force could volunteer for the Home Guard or become an air raid warden.

THE HOME GUARD

The Home Guard was made up of men who were trained to protect their towns or villages from invasion. At first, they were armed with whatever they could get hold of – old shot guns, knives and even broom handles.

WATCHERS AND WARDENS

At night, fire watchers looked out for fires and air raid wardens patrolled the streets checking that no light was escaping from the blackout curtains. After a long night shift, they often had to go to work the next day.

Eileen remembers that even in the country everyone played their part.

> *Several nights a week my older cousin had to put on her Auxiliary Fire Service uniform and sleep at the fire station to run the station. Women operated the phones but did not fight the fires.*

A training session in Hertfordshire for members of the Post Office Home Guard.

PENNIES FOR SPITFIRES
Cynthia's primary school joined in the war effort and started to save £5,000 for a Spitfire fighter aircraft.

↑ Cynthia's primary school was still saving for a Spitfire when she left to go to the high school in 1940.

> *A Polish airman came to thank us for our efforts and to talk about the war. We learnt the Polish National Anthem to welcome him – in Polish – and practised until we were word and note perfect. I can still sing it today. He told us that freedom was the most precious gift and that now he was fighting with his British brothers and sisters for the freedom of Poland.*

SALVAGE
Materials were hard to obtain for the factories busy producing weapons and ammunition. Nothing went to waste. Everything metal, from old kettles to iron railings, was salvaged. This meant it was collected and recycled into shells, guns, ships, tanks and aircraft.

Spies!
Posters with such slogans as 'Careless Talk Costs Lives' and 'Tell Nobody, Not Even Her' warned everyone to be on their guard all the time – anybody could be a spy!

CARELESS TALK COSTS LIVES

you never know who's listening!

! Eileen remembers...
"There was excitement in Malvern when we heard that one of the matrons from another school had been caught signalling with a torch at night on the Malvern Hills to help the Germans."

← Valerie, Cynthia's eight-year-old cousin, painted this picture showing how useful salvage was.

Bill Mellow's story

Bill, 1941

NAVY COMMANDO

Bill joined the navy as a boy of 16, in 1936. In 1939, when war broke out, Bill was on a minesweeper in Gibraltar. Seven months later, he trained as a navy commando.

❝ *As commandos we were highly trained in street fighting, house clearing, setting booby traps and wet landings. We did obstacle courses and once a month we did a 45-mile [72-kilometre] route march carrying a 30-pound [14-kilogram] pack, rifles and Bren guns.* ❞

COMMANDO RAID

Bill's first commando raid was behind the enemy front line at Bardiyah on the North African coast. The plan was to attack the Italian and German barracks.

❝ *Our job was to silence the sentries and wreck the place. The officers' place was laid for breakfast, we wrecked that and then blew the lock gate of their reservoir – their fresh water – and emptied that, and then set a big store dump alight, loaded with big lorry tyres and car tyres.*

Some of the men didn't make it back to the beach on time and we had to leave them behind. We never knew what happened to them. We heard on Rome radio that if any more British commandos were caught, they would be shot. ❞

⬆ After the war, Bill trained junior seamen. His young (15 and 16 year old) trainees put on this impressive display in 1953.

RAID ON DIEPPE

In August 1942 Bill was involved in a raid on Dieppe in France. His job was to take commandos into shore. The Germans started to fire mortars at them and one went under his landing craft, separating the shaft from the engine. The craft started to drift, but Bill felt they were being looked after that day.

> *A gap appeared in the smoke, and steaming along was a little submarine chaser. It saw our plight and came belting through ... they threw me a line and towed me out the other side of the smoke.*

As they were being towed away from Dieppe, they were attacked twice. Above them they saw a Spitfire hit by enemy fire.

> *The Spitfire went down. We could see it under the water but there was nothing we could do. I could have cried for the fellow.*

A SURPRISE VISIT

At last they got back to Newhaven and to safety. Bill visited his aunt who lived along the coast.

> *She came to the door, and I said, 'Hello' and she nearly collapsed. Her eyes lit up. She said 'Billy! Ah, what's happened to you?' So I said, 'Nothing really,' and she said, 'You'd better ring your mum.' The phone at home only went once and it was answered. My mum was there – she'd been listening to the news on the radio and was worried about me.*

After the war, Bill stayed in the navy until he retired.

⬇ Soldiers prepare to leave France after the raid on Dieppe, 1942.

The ones left behind

Many people were parted from their loved-ones for long periods. They had to wait and hope that they would come home safely.

CHRISTMAS ON LEAVE

The first Christmas Bill spent at home during the war, everybody made a big fuss of him. But his mum was afraid for him. She took him aside.

> " *My mum said, 'Look, come out of this commando business!' I said, 'Why?' She said, 'They'll catch up with you!' I said, 'They'll have to run fast if they do.' She said, 'No, tell them you don't like it.' I said, 'I can't do that!' She never did like it. I loved it. I was single then. Oh yes, I really loved it.* "

↑ Friends and family wave off servicemen at Paddington station, London in 1942.

British death toll

Military	326,000
Civilian	62,000
Total deaths	388,000

(!) Eileen remembers...
"I remember going to the station to see off the very young men who had been called up. Everyone went."

MISUNDERSTANDINGS

It was difficult for those left behind to understand what being in the forces was really like. Bill's mother tried to send a parcel.

> *My mother thought she'd send me a Christmas parcel. So they killed one of the cockerels, cooked it and packed some fruit as well and sent me a parcel – well I got it about three or four months later. It was nearly walking. So it went straight in the bin – whoar!*

Bill (left) and Eric, 1938

Everyone tried to be supportive but misunderstandings often happened. Bill could not keep in touch all the time.

> *I used to get told off for not writing, but I wasn't always in a position to write. My fiancée got so annoyed that she sent the ring back to me. I just walked out on the upper deck and I threw the ring over the side.*

CODES

Letters were read and cut by the censors in case any important military secrets were given away, and sometimes it was months before any post arrived.

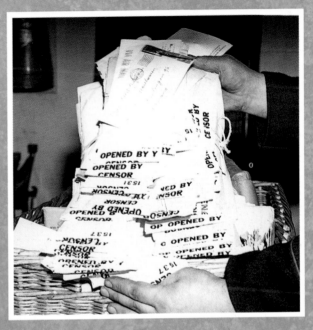

↑ Letters ready for delivery after being opened and examined by postal censors.

Meg remembers...
"My two brothers used to send letters back to my father with a code. The letter at the beginning of every sentence was the leading letter of the place they were in. My father had a large map and used to mark out all of the places where they were."

Amy remembers...
"I remember my fiancé Gerry saying, 'I'm going overseas and I'll make out a code so you and Mum will know where I am.' We thought – how clever of him. When we got the letter, we laughed because it had 'Gibraltar' written across the top – and that's where he was!"

Women's Land Army

Meg Stone's story

Meg, 1944

'We could do with thousands more like you..'

JOIN THE
WOMEN'S LAND ARMY

⬆ By 1944 there were 80,000 women in the Land Army.

LAND GIRL

The Women's Land Army was set up because women were needed to work on farms to replace the men who had been called up. Meg's family didn't want her to join the women's branches of the army, navy or air force, but they approved of the Land Army. So Meg joined the Land Army and became a 'land girl'.

HARD WORK

Although Meg lived in the country, she hadn't done farm work before. She wasn't given any special training and she was expected to work as hard as the men. Her day started at 4.30 in the morning. If Meg was working in the fields, she would be with a gang of men. If she was hedging or ditching – digging ditches – she worked with just one man.

> *We did what the men did. We carried a hundredweight [50 kilograms] – mostly a sack of feed or a bale of hay or straw. You had to get it up on your back. It was a knack.*

WORKING WITH COWS

Although Meg loved animals, she was afraid of cows.

> *My first boss said, 'You'd better learn to milk.' 'Oh no,' I said, 'I'm terrified of cows!' 'Well that's what the country needs,' he said. So that's what I did. I completely overcame my fear. I remember the farmer standing over me saying, 'Go on, go for it!' which made your hands really ache until you got used to it .*

BATH TIME

Meg slept at the farms where she was working. Usually even having a bath was hard work.

> " *I carried the hot water upstairs, tipped it in the bath (it just covered the bottom), and added enough cold water to cool it – but it was probably cold by that time anyway. During the war, you were only allowed five inches [13 centimetres] of water in your bath.* "

⬇ The land girls did all the jobs on the farm that the men did. This land girl in Kent has been issued with a steel helmet because of flying bombs.

D-DAY LANDINGS

Meg remembers when one of the main events of the war affected the peaceful countryside, although she didn't know what was going on at the time.

> " *We lived quite near Harwell where there was a big aerodrome. One day we were up there and saw miles of gliders all over the grass. The next day there were none. They had all gone for the D-Day landings and of course didn't come back.* "

After the war, Meg spent some time working on farms in Australia. Back in England, she married a farmer and has lived on a farm ever since.

23

Women and the war

NEW CHALLENGES

Women were affected by the war in many different ways. Mothers, sisters and wives were left behind when the men were called up, but there were new jobs open to them and new challenges to be faced at home.

VOLUNTEERS

Women could volunteer to become air raid wardens and fire watchers. The WVS, the Women's Voluntary Service, set up mobile canteens for rescue workers during air raids. They distributed clothes and household items to people who had lost their homes in air raids.

⬇ Women worked in every branch of the armed forces.

➡ Women replaced the men in factories, often doing heavy and dangerous jobs, including munitions work.

WOMEN OF BRITAIN
COME INTO THE FACTORIES
ASK AT ANY EMPLOYMENT EXCHANGE FOR ADVICE AND FULL DETAILS

TEACHERS AND NURSES

Retired teachers and women who had left teaching when they got married returned to work. Many women trained as nurses and went to work in field hospitals to care for the wounded.

HOUSEWIVES

Housewives had the difficult task of feeding and clothing their families with food and clothes coupons. They looked after neighbours' children, allowing other mothers to work in essential jobs, and they took in evacuees.

THE FORCES

Women could join the women's branches of the army – the Auxiliary Territorial Service (ATS), the navy – the Women's Royal Naval Service (WRNS) and the air force – the Women's Auxiliary Air Force (WAAF). Many, like Meg, joined the Land Army.

ATS AT THE WHEEL

Ceaselessly new vehicles roll off the production lines. Army units await them, the ATS deliver them

WOMEN'S · ROYAL · NAVAL · SERVICE

join the **Wrens**

...D · FREE · A · MAN · FOR · THE · FLEET

APPLY TO DIRECTOR W.R.N.S. ADMIRALTY S.W.1.
OR THE NEAREST EMPLOYMENT EXCHANGE

When the war was over, Meg felt that the Women's Land Army was overlooked.

> 66 *When they had processions for the Armistice in London, the forces and everybody else were represented, but land girls were not.* 99

War weddings

Couples who got married during the war were often separated almost immediately after the wedding. Bill and his fiancée Margaret made up after their misunderstanding and their wedding plans were on again.

"*My sister got married and Margaret was one of the bridesmaids. After the wedding she flung her arms round my neck and said, 'Let's make it up'. And we did. We got married in May 1945 just as the war in Europe was ending. A month later, I was on my way to India.*"

⬆ Bill and Margaret have been married for 57 years.

Yet Meg found that life in the Land Army was not an easy option.

> 66 *We worked harder physically and probably longer hours and had far less holidays in the Land Army than I would have done in the ATS.* 99

⬆ Amy and Gerry: "We were only married three months before he went overseas for two and half years."

Amy met Gerry who was in the RAF when they were stationed at the same aerodrome.

"*We were travelling on the train from Oxford to London and there was an air raid. We sat in this blacked-out train with bombs falling all over the place. The sky was lit up with searchlights. It was very moving and frightening. To my utter astonishment, Gerry asked me to marry him. Could you think of any-thing more romantic? 'Oh!' I said, 'Yes.'*"

The Auxiliary Territorial Service (ATS)

Amy, 1942

⬇ Women of the WAAF plotting the course of planes. The ATS and the WAAF shared this task.

JOINING UP

Amy was living at home and working at the Overseas Telephone Exchange in Liverpool when the war touched her in a very personal way. She received some bad news.

> *The boyfriend I had at the time had just sailed to Singapore. Before they could get off the boat, the Japanese had taken them prisoners. I couldn't stand it any longer. I joined the ATS.*

ATS

The ATS supported the army. Amy's job was plotting searchlights.

> *You may have seen it in films – girls with long sticks with maps in front of them. Information came through our headphones about German planes coming in and our fighters going up after them. We followed what was going on and plotted on our map where the searchlights would go.*

HARD WORK

We worked from dusk to dawn, all of us saying, 'When this war is over, we'll have a bed in every room.' We were permanently tired.

THE AMERICANS ARRIVE

The ops (operations) room was the holy of holies. You didn't speak, you did your job and you got on with it. The Americans came in 1942–3 and they took over the ops room and it was like a circus. They were so noisy, which we were thrilled about. I don't think it was ever the same again.

DANCES

We used to have all sorts of dances in the village hall called Wings for Victory dances. I loved dancing. The Americans taught us a dance called the Jitterbug. One of the girls – Ethel – went under the legs and over the top – I used to go just to watch her.

→ The jitterbug was an acrobatic and very energetic dance.

MARCHING

Amy was good at dancing, but she wasn't so good at marching.

When I was promoted, I had to teach drill. The thing that horrified me was changing step on the march. You had to get it on the right foot for them to change otherwise it was absolute chaos! The instructress said, 'It isn't your best point is it, Amy?'

War is over!

VE DAY

The Germans surrendered, and on 8th May 1945 parties were held all over the country to celebrate VE (Victory in Europe) Day.

CELEBRATIONS IN LONDON

Amy was on leave and her mother and younger brother, Peter, came down from Liverpool to meet her in London for the VE celebrations.

> *I wasn't in uniform, and this upset my mother enormously. She wanted to be proud of me. There were crowds and crowds of people. Everybody you could think of was in London celebrating and singing and it was fantastic.*

> *My mother was a great monarchist. She said, 'Would it be a good idea if we went to Buckingham Palace?'*
>
> *The Royal Family came out on the balcony with Winston Churchill. That made my mother's day. I thought she was going to die of happiness. She was there on one of the most memorable days of history.*

⬇ Acknowledging the crowds on VE Day. From left to right: Princess Elizabeth, Queen Elizabeth, the Prime Minister Winston Churchill, King George VI, Princess Margaret.

TEARS AND LAUGHTER
It was a time of rejoicing but also one of sadness for the terrible losses.

> *The tears rolled down my face. I realised what it meant to my mother and I wished I'd been wearing my uniform.*
>
> *People were rejoicing and people were crying, saying, 'I lost my son' – 'We were bombed out'. They wanted to tell you these things.*

↓ Street parties were held throughout the country.

! Meg remembers...
"We all went into Axminster to celebrate. We were all dancing in the square, letting our hair down. It was great fun and I kissed all the wrong people."

Victory in Japan

In August 1945, President Truman of the United States gave the order for two atomic bombs to be dropped on Japan. The bombs caused such terrible devastation that the Japanese surrendered unconditionally on 2nd September. Finally, the war was over.

↓ Japan's surrender marked the end of the war.

DAILY EXPRESS

Attlee, at midnight, gives news that it is all over

PEACE ON EARTH

JAPS REPLY: We have the honour to surrender. Mikado orders all his Forces to cease fire

TERMS ACCEPTED—AND NO CONDITIONS

Tears flow at Sublime Palace

PETAIN TO DIE

GOING HOME
At the end of the war, Bill was in India. He was impatient to get home, but progress was infuriatingly slow.

> *We brought this old liner home which had been lent to the Indian navy. It took us ages. We kept breaking down, but we made it eventually. I rang my mum. Margaret was working down the road in the Post Office. I said, tell Marg I'm home. When I rang up again, Marg was waiting and oh, she was over the moon.*

REBUILDING
After the celebrations were over, men and women who had served in the forces handed in their uniforms and returned to ordinary life. Throughout the country, people had pulled together to fight for freedom. Now the war had been won, people wanted to rebuild Britain into a better place for everyone to live in.

Timeline

1939

1st June The Women's Land Army, originally created in World War I, is revived for volunteers.

August Evacuation of children from cities to the countryside begins.

1st September German troops invade Poland.

3rd September Britain and France declare war on Germany.

December Food rationing is introduced.

1940

1st January Two million men between the ages of 19 and 27 are called up.

10th May Winston Churchill takes over from Neville Chamberlain as Prime Minister.

June 338,226 British troops are evacuated from Dunkirk in northern France.

11th June Italy declares war on Britain and France.

14th June German troops march into Paris.

23rd July The Home Guard is set up.

August – October The Royal Air Force fights the German Luftwaffe in the Battle of Britain.

7 September The Blitz starts – German aircraft bomb British cities.

1941

22nd January The North African port of Tobruk is captured by Allied troops.

27th May The 'unsinkable' German battleship *The Bismark* is sunk.

June Germany invades Russia.

July Japan invades South-East Asia.

December Single women aged 19 to 30, with no children, are called up to work in war industries, the Land Army and the armed forces.

7th December Japan attacks American navy in Pearl Harbor – America joins in the war.

1942

March The RAF launches air raids on ports and industrial centres in Germany.

19th August Many British and Allied troops are killed in the Dieppe raid.

1943

31st January Russians defeat the Germans in the siege of Stalingrad.

17th May Bouncing bombs destroy dams on German rivers.

8th September Italy surrenders to the Allies.

1944

6th June D-Day, Allied troops land on the Normandy beaches and invade Europe.

25th August Paris is liberated.

1945

14th February German city of Dresden is destroyed in one night of bombing.

30th April The Allies take Berlin. Hitler commits suicide.

April The full horror of German concentration camps (for the detention of prisoners, especially Jews) discovered.

8th May VE (Victory in Europe) Day.

6th and 9th August Atom bombs dropped on Japan, killing more than 150,000 people.

14th August Japan surrenders. VJ (Victory in Japan) Day is celebrated.

Glossary

Aerodrome The buildings, runways and surrounding land from which aeroplanes take off and land.

Allied Forces The Allies were the countries Britain and its colonies, USA and Canada and the USSR that fought together against Germany, Italy and Japan. The forces were the army, navy and air force of each country.

Ambassador A high-ranking person whose job is to represent their country abroad.

Auxiliary A worker who supports others in their job. Women in the Auxiliary Territorial Service supported the army during the war.

Barracks A building where members of the forces or other workers sleep and live.

Blitz Short for Blitzkrieg – a German word meaning 'lightning war'. The German bombing of British cities was called the Blitz.

Bren gun A type of light machine gun.

Cabinet A group of ministers led by the Prime Minister which meets to discuss how the government runs the country. During World War II, a War Cabinet made decisions about running the war.

Call-up A government order to join the armed forces.

Code Letters, numbers and symbols which are used to hide secret information.

Dictator A ruler who has absolute power. Adolf Hitler was a dictator in Germany during World War II.

Hamlet A very small village.

Invasion When armed forces of one country go into another country to take it over.

Military Anything to do with the armed forces.

Monarchist Someone who enthusiastically supports their king or queen.

Munitions Weapons, ammunition such as rockets and bullets and fighting equipment.

Plotting Putting markers on a map or chart to show the position of something.

Radar Radio detection and ranging. A system of using radio signals to detect the exact position of objects such as aircraft.

Rationing A system allowing people a certain amount of food, clothing or fuel used during World War II and afterwards.

Searchlight A very bright light used to search for and light up enemy aircraft in the night sky.

Sentry A soldier on guard whose job is to keep a look out for danger.

Telephone exchange A building where telephone operators receive and direct telephone calls.

Index